EXCEL: FORMULAS & FUNCTIONS

ABOUT THIS BOOK

Excel: Formulas and Functions is for people who have a basic understanding of Excel 2000, including how to enter and format data, select cells, save workbooks, and rename worksheets.

ALTHOUGH MANY PEOPLE USE EXCEL simply to create and manage lists or for its charting features, the real power of the program lies in its use as a calculating tool and for analyzing and manipulating data. To make best use of these features, you need to know about formulas and functions; explaining how to use these is the object of this book.

The opening chapter provides a brief overview of Excel's scope as a calculating tool. Chapters two and three explain how to create and edit formulas and link data within and between worksheets. The vital topic of copying formulas and the different types of cell references that can be used in formulas are also covered. Chapter four explains what an Excel function is and works through the use of several different types – for example, financial and logical functions. The final chapter explains common errors and how to fix them.

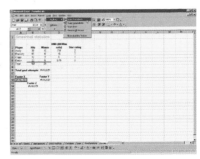

Throughout this book, information is presented using step-by-step sequences. Virtually every step is accompanied by an illustration showing how your screen should look at each stage. Command keys, such as ENTER and CTRL, are shown in these rectangles: [Enter←] and [Ctrl], to avoid confusion, for example, over whether you should press that key or type the letters "ctrl." Cross-references are shown in the text as left- and right-hand page icons: ◁ and ▷. The page number and the title of the paragraph to which you are referred are shown at the foot of the page.

As well as the step-by-step sections, there are boxes that explain particular features in detail, and tip boxes that provide alternative methods and shortcuts. Finally, at the back of the book, you will find a glossary of terms commonly used in the context of formulas and functions and a comprehensive index.

ESSENTIAL DK COMPUTERS

SPREADSHEETS

EXCEL: FORMULAS & FUNCTIONS

ROBERT DINWIDDIE

LONDON, NEW YORK, MUNICH,
MELBOURNE, AND DELHI

SENIOR EDITOR Jacky Jackson
SENIOR ART EDITOR Sarah Cowley
US EDITORS Gary Werner and Margaret Parrish
DTP DESIGNER Julian Dams
PRODUCTION CONTROLLER Michelle Thomas

MANAGING EDITOR Adèle Hayward
SENIOR MANAGING ART EDITOR Karen Self

Produced for Dorling Kindersley Limited by
Design Revolution Limited, Queens Park Villa,
30 West Drive, Brighton, England BN2 2GE
EDITORIAL DIRECTOR Ian Whitelaw
SENIOR DESIGNER Andrew Easton
PROJECT EDITOR Julie Whitaker
DESIGNER Paul Bowler

First American Edition, 2002

04 05 10 9 8 7 6 5 4

Published in the United States by
DK Publishing, Inc.
375 Hudson Street
New York, NY 10014

DK Publishing offers special discounts for bulk purchases for sales promotions or
premiums. Specific, large-quantity needs can be met with special editions, including
personalized covers, excerpts of existing guides, and corporate imprints.
For more information, contact Special Markets Department, DK Publishing, Inc.,
95 Madison Ave., New York, NY 10016 Fax: 800-600-9098.

A Cataloging in Publication record is available from the Library of Congress.

ISBN 0-7894-8410-2

Color reproduced by Colourscan, Singapore
Printed in China

see our complete product line at
www.dk.com

CONTENTS

MICROSOFT EXCEL

Excel belongs to the group of computer applications known as spreadsheets, which are designed to help you record, analyze, manipulate, and present quantitative information.

EXCEL AS A CALCULATING TOOL

At the most basic level, running Excel is very similar to using a sophisticated electronic calculator. As with a calculator, you can carry out calculations, store the results in memory areas, and then recall these at a later stage. But most calculators offer only a handful of memory areas for storing data, whereas each Excel worksheet provides over 15 million such areas (the number of cells in a worksheet). Also, in Excel, many separately memorized pieces of data can be viewed together.

AN EXCEL WORKSHEET

Each Excel worksheet has the capacity for holding millions of separate pieces of data and each of these can be linked with others by means of formulas. Furthermore, when you change some data, any linked pieces of data are updated immediately.

	A	B	C	D	E	F	G	H	I	J
1	**WIZZKIDD ACCOUNT AT MEGABANK**									
2										
3	**Date**	**Item**	**Income**	**Expenditure**	**Balance**		**Recurring items**			
4	1-Aug	Paycheck	$ 2,128.00		$ 2,128.00		Paycheck	$2,128.00		
5	4-Aug	Rent		$ 921.00	$ 1,207.00		Rent	$ 921.00		
6	20-Aug	Phone bill		$ 55.00	$ 1,152.00		Phone bill	$ 55.00		
7	23-Aug	Cash withdrawal		$ 350.00	$ 802.00					
8	29-Aug	Check from Grandma	$ 60.00		$ 862.00					
9	1-Sep	Paycheck	$ 2,128.00		$ 2,990.00					
10	4-Sep	Rent		$ 921.00	$ 2,069.00					
11	10-Sep	Stock investments		$ 2,029.00	$ 40.00					
12	18-Sep	Cash from Steve	$ 20.00							
13	20-Sep	Phone bill		$ 55.00	$ (15.00)					
14	1-Oct	Paycheck	$ 2,128.00		$ 2,113.00					
15	2-Oct	Cash for Steve		$ 21.00						
16	4-Oct	Rent		$ 921.00	$ 1,192.00					
17	20-Oct	Phone bill		$ 55.00	$ 1,137.00					

USES OF FORMULAS AND FUNCTIONS

All calculations in Excel rely on the use of formulas. These vary from relatively simple arithmetic instructions to complex "recipes" for combining and manipulating data that has already been entered into a worksheet. Excel functions are ready-made little programs or calculation tools that can be incorporated into formulas. The two examples given below will give you a flavor of some of the uses of the formulas and functions that will be explained later in this book.

FINANCIAL MODELING

On pages 21–29, you will find out how you can use a simple copied Excel formula to create a bank account model. This can be used to project and monitor a running balance over several months, which can be useful for personal financial planning.

STATISTICAL ANALYSIS

Excel provides hundreds of functions that can be used to speed up statistical analysis of data and other types of "number-crunching." Some example functions are covered on pages 46–55.

THE EXCEL WINDOW

Soon after you launch Microsoft Excel, a window called **Microsoft Excel – Book1** appears. At the center of the window is a worksheet – a grid of blank rectangular cells. Letters and numbers label the columns and rows of the grid. Each cell has an address (such as E3), which is the column and row in which it is found.

THE EXCEL WINDOW

❶ Title bar
Title of the active workbook.

❷ Menu bar
Contains the main menus for frequently used commands.

❸ Formula bar
What you enter in the active cell also appears here.

❹ Standard toolbar
These buttons carry out frequently used actions.

❺ Formatting toolbar
Options for changing data presentation.

❻ Column header buttons
Click on the header button to select the whole column.

❼ Row header buttons
Click on the row header to select the entire row.

❽ Active cell
Whatever you type appears in the active cell.

❾ Worksheet tabs
Workbooks contain worksheets – click to select one.

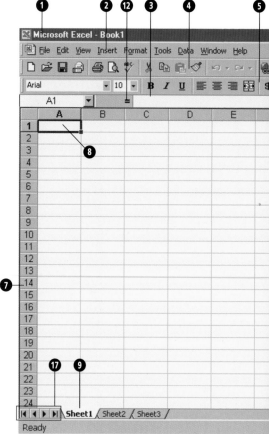

TOOLBAR LAYOUT

If Excel doesn't show the formatting toolbar below the standard toolbar, place the cursor over the formatting toolbar

"handle." When the four-headed arrow appears, (right) hold down the mouse button and "drag" the toolbar into position.

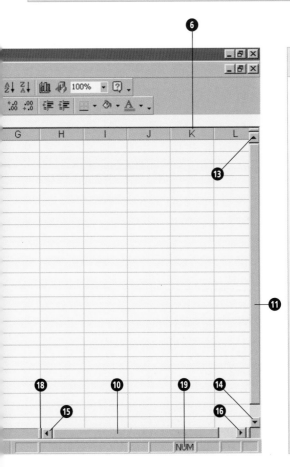

THE EXCEL WINDOW

❿ Horizontal scroll bar
To scroll horizontally through the worksheet.

⓫ Vertical scroll bar
To scroll vertically through the worksheet.

⓬ = button
Used to start entering a formula in a cell.

⓭ Scroll-up arrow
Move up the worksheet.

⓮ Scroll-down arrow
Move down the worksheet.

⓯ Left-scroll arrow
Scrolls the sheet to the left.

⓰ Right-scroll arrow
Scrolls the sheet to the right.

⓱ Tab scrolling buttons
Scroll through the sheets if they cannot all be displayed.

⓲ Tab split box
Click and drag to show tabs or to increase the scroll bar.

⓳ NUM lock
Shows that the numeric keypad on the right of the keyboard is on.

Using the = Button

THE TWO MAIN EXCEL TOOLBARS

Many of the actions, or commands, that you want to perform on data can be carried out by clicking on toolbar buttons. When you launch Excel, the standard toolbar and the formatting toolbar are the usual toolbars displayed. They contain buttons whose actions are described below. The standard toolbar contains buttons for actions as diverse as opening a new workbook or undoing an action. The formatting toolbar contains buttons for changing the worksheet's appearance.

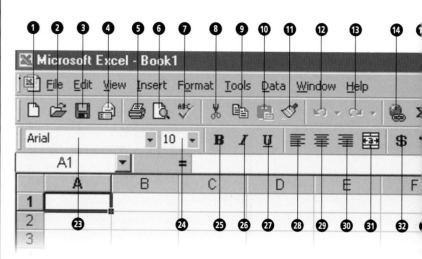

BUTTON FUNCTIONS

1. New workbook
2. Open file
3. Save workbook
4. Email workbook/sheet
5. Print
6. Print preview
7. Spelling checker
8. Cut
9. Copy
10. Paste
11. Format painter
12. Undo action(s)
13. Redo action(s)
14. Insert hyperlink
15. AutoSum
16. Paste function
17. Sort ascending
18. Sort descending
19. Chart wizard
20. Drawing toolbar
21. Zoom view
22. Help
23. Font selector
24. Font size selector

 44 The AutoSum Button

46 Using the Function Wizard

CUSTOMIZING A TOOLBAR

Click the arrow at the far right of the formatting toolbar, then on the arrow on the **Add or Remove Buttons** box that appears. A drop-down menu opens from which you can add or remove toolbar buttons.

ScreenTips

It isn't necessary to memorize all these buttons. Roll the cursor over a button, wait for a second, and a ScreenTip appears telling you the function of the button.

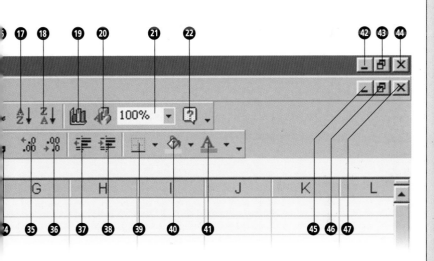

BUTTON FUNCTIONS

- ㉕ Bold
- ㉖ Italic
- ㉗ Underline
- ㉘ Align left
- ㉙ Center
- ㉚ Align right
- ㉛ Merge and center
- ㉜ Currency style
- ㉝ Percent style
- ㉞ Comma style
- ㉟ Increase decimals
- ㊱ Decrease decimals
- ㊲ Decrease indent
- ㊳ Increase indent
- ㊴ Add/remove borders
- ㊵ Fill color
- ㊶ Font color
- ㊷ Minimize Excel
- ㊸ Restore Excel
- ㊹ Close Excel
- ㊺ Minimize worksheet
- ㊻ Restore worksheet
- ㊼ Close worksheet

HOW FORMULAS WORK

All calculations in Excel rely on expressions called formulas that are entered into worksheet cells. To use Excel effectively as a calculating tool, you need to understand how formulas work.

UNDERSTANDING FORMULA BASICS

A formula is an expression that instructs Excel to calculate a value for a worksheet cell by performing a particular operation on some specified data. Every Excel formula begins with an equals sign (=). Following the equals sign are the pieces of data to be combined or calculated (called operands). These are separated by calculation operators, such as + (add), - (subtract), or * (multiply). The operands are usually numbers or other types of data that you have typed into the formula, or are references to other worksheet cells. An Excel formula can range from a simple addition to a long expression instructing Excel to combine many pieces of data in a complex way. Try creating a few formulas, starting with a very simple one.

1 **A VERY SIMPLE FORMULA**

● Open a new workbook, save it as **Formulas.xls**, select cell B2 in Sheet1, and type the expression **=5+3** into the cell. In this simple formula, you are instructing Excel to add the numbers 5 and 3. The numbers "5" and "3" are the operands, and + (addition) is the operator that you are applying to these operands.

● Press Enter↵ and look
at cell B2. It now contains
the value **8** – the result of
adding together 5 and 3.

● Now click on cell B2
again and look in the
formula bar (the extended
white space immediately
above the worksheet). It
contains the formula
=5+3. If you ever want to
know whether a cell
contains a formula (and
what that formula is), just
click on the cell and look
in the formula bar.

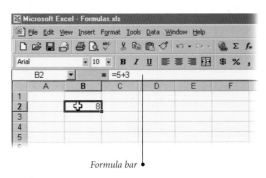

Formula bar ●

2 A LONGER FORMULA

● Now select cell C2 and
type the formula **=(68-
3)/(9+4)**. This tells Excel to
subtract 3 from 68 and then
divide the result by the sum
of 9 and 4. In this formula,
there are four operands (the
numbers) and three opera-
tors (-, +, and /). The parentheses tell Excel what order
to carry out the operations
in the formula (the
subtraction and addition
first, then the division).

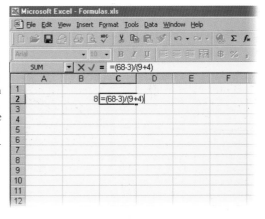

● Press Enter↵. Cell C2
should now display the
result of the calculation as
5 (65 divided by 13).

EXCEL CALCULATION OPERATORS

The main arithmetic operators used in the Excel program are + (add), - (subtract), * (multiply), / (divide), and ^ (raise to the power of). Below, you will find a summary of these operators.

OPERATOR	MEANING	EXAMPLE FORMULA	VALUE CALCULATED BY EXAMPLE
+	Add	=2+3	5
-	Subtract	=10-4	6
*	Multiply	=5*4	20
/	Divide	=18/3	6
^	Raise to the power of	=3^3	27 (3^3)

CALCULATION ORDER

Excel follows a set order in calculations within a formula. Exponential operations are done first, then multiplication and division, then addition and subtraction. For example, consider the formula =3+6*3^2. To calculate the result of this formula as it stands, Excel would first calculate 3^2, which means 3^2, giving 9. It then multiplies this by 6 (giving 54), and then adds the result to 3 (giving a final result of 57). If you wanted the operations to occur in a different order, you would need to use parentheses. For example, if you used parentheses as follows =(3+6)*3^2, the operation in parentheses would be done first and the final result would be 81 (9×3^2).

CELL CONTENT AND VALUE

A cell's content and its value are not always the same. Its content is the text, numerical expression, or formula that has been typed into it and can be checked by clicking on the cell and looking in the formula bar. Its value is what you see in the cell on-screen. When a cell contains a formula, its content comprises that formula (for example, =5+3), but what you see in the cell is the value calculated by that formula (for example, 8).

3 USING CELL REFERENCES

● So far, the operands you have used in your formulas have been numbers that you have typed directly into the formulas. Excel is very useful for performing calculations of this sort, but its real power derives from using existing data in the worksheet as operands. This is done by means of cell references. These tell Excel to use the values in particular cells as operands.

● Select cell D2 and type the formula **=B2*C2**. This tells Excel to take the existing value in B2, multiply it by the value in C2, and display the result in D2. The operands "B2" and "C2" are references to the values of the cells B2 and C2.

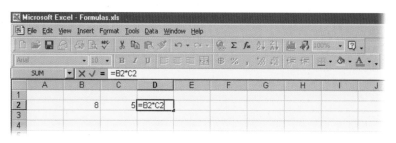

● Press Enter↵ and you should see that cell D2 now has the value **40** (the result of multiplying 8 by 5).

● Now double-click on cell D2. The double-click displays the formula =B2*C2 within the cell itself. Note that the two cells referenced by the formula are displayed with colored borders and that the same colors have been used to display the cell reference operands (B2 and C2) in cell D2. This color-coding is helpful in revealing how a formula has been constructed.

4 UPDATING A REFERENCED CELL

● Now let's see what happens if you change the value of a cell that has been referenced by a formula elsewhere on a worksheet.

● Double-click in cell B2 to select it, and type **5** to replace its existing contents.

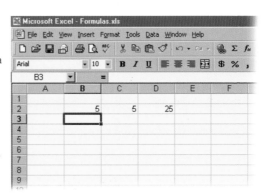

● Press [Enter←]. As the value of B2 updates to 5, note that the value of D2, which contains the formula =B2*C2, also updates, to 25. Whenever a change occurs to the value of a worksheet cell, Excel automatically updates the value of any cell that references the changed cell.

THE POWER OF AUTOMATIC RECALCULATION

One of Excel's most useful features is that when the value of a cell changes, the program automatically recalculates any other cell containing a formula that references the updated cell. It also recalculates the value of any further cells that reference the cells that referenced the updated cell … and so on. This means that an Excel worksheet (or several worksheets) can be used to build up a mathematical "model" of, for example, a family's finances or a scientific study based on a number of variable values and a series of formulas. The effects on the model of small alterations to the variables can then be seen instantly.

CREATING AND EDITING FORMULAS

Formulas are so fundamentally basic to carrying out calculations in Excel that it makes it worthwhile to learn some tips and tricks for entering them into worksheet cells. Once a formula has been entered, it can be edited just like the contents of any other worksheet cell. Try practicing the following techniques.

1 POINTING AND CLICKING

● Click on cell B4. In this cell, you want to enter a formula that will multiply together the values in cells B2, C2, and D2. But you don't actually have to type in the formula =B2*C2*D2. You can enter the cell references by pointing and clicking with your mouse.
● Start off by typing in an equals (=) sign.

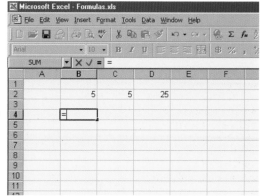

● Now click on cell B2. You will see that the cell's address (B2) is automatically added to the formula that you are constructing in B4.

● Now type an asterisk (*) and then click on cell C2. This is then added to the formula in B4.

● Type * again and click on cell D2. Then press Enter ↵ to complete the formula.

	A	B	C	D	E	F
SUM	▼	× ✓	=	=B2*C2*D2		
1						
2		5	5	25		
3						

● Cell B4 should now have the value **625** (5 x 5 x 25).

	A	B	C	D	E	F
1						
2		5	5	25		
3						
4		625				
5						

2 USING THE = BUTTON

● Another helpful device is the "=" button, which can be found just to the left of the formula bar 🗅.
● Select cell B6 and then click on the = button.

= button   *Formula bar*

B6	▼	=				
	A	B	C	D	E	F
1						
2		5	5	25		
3						
4		625				
5						
6						
7						

● An = is automatically inserted to start the formula. Also, a special panel containing the words **Formula result** = appears below the formula bar.

| Arial | ▼ | 10 | ▼ | B | I | U | | | | | $ | % | , |

SUM	▼	× ✓	=	=		
?	Formula result =				OK	Can
2		5	5	25		
3						
4		625				
5						
6		=				
7						

● Click on cell B4 to insert this cell reference into the formula, then type **/10+7**. As you add new operands, the formula result calculation continually updates to show the value that will result from the formula.

SUM	▼	× ✓	=	=B4/10+7		
?	Formula result =69.5				OK	Can
2		5	5	25		
3						
4		625				
5						
6		=B4/10+7				
7						

🗅 ⓬ = **button**

● Finally press [Enter ←] or click on the **OK** button to complete the formula. The calculation result in this instant should be **69.5**.

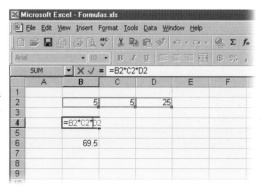

3 IN-CELL EDITING

● You can alter a formula either by in-cell editing or by editing the formula in the formula bar. First, try in-cell editing. Suppose you want to change the formula in cell B4.

● Double-click on cell B4. The formula =**B2*C2*D2** now appears in the cell. Point and click just after the second asterisk.

● Press [← Bksp] to remove the asterisk and type + to add a plus sign instead.

● Press [Enter ←] and the value in cell B4 should now be **50**. The value of cell B6, which contains a formula that references B4, also updates, to **12**.

4 EDITING IN THE FORMULA BAR

Formula bar

- Another way of editing a formula is to perform the alteration in the formula bar.

- Single-click on cell B4, point the mouse pointer at the formula in the formula bar and click immediately after the remaining asterisk.

- Press `← Bksp` to delete the asterisk, type / (forward slash) to indicate division, so the formula now reads =B2/C2+D2.

- Press `Enter ↵` and the value in cell B4 should now be **26** (simultaneously the value in B6 updates to **9.6**).

Avoid a mouse click!

When you are manually editing a formula, avoid inadvertently clicking with the mouse anywhere on the worksheet. If you do, the address of the cell that you clicked on will automatically be inserted into the formula, which you will usually not want.

RECOGNIZING ERROR MESSAGES

After you have entered a formula into a cell, you may sometimes get an error message saying that the formula is invalid. In this case, Excel usually provides a suggestion as to what you may have meant to enter. If you see any of the following in a cell: #DIV/0!, #VALUE!, #NULL!, #NUM!, #REF!, #NAME?, ######, or #N/A, these indicate specific types of problems ⌐.

COPYING FORMULAS: A BANK BALANCE PROJECTION

Formulas can be copied from one cell to another like any other cell contents – and copying formulas can be a particularly smart way of using them. In this section, you are going to create a checking account register in Excel and project the bank balance into the future using a copied formula. Many people find it difficult to keep track of their banking transactions and, as a result, inadvertently exceed overdraft limits, incurring unwanted charges. Setting up a checking account register in Excel, and spending a few minutes each week maintaining it, can save money! In the practical example, you will be modeling the account of a certain Joe Wizzkidd, but you can apply the same techniques to your own situation.

1 SETTING UP A REGISTER

● Joe Wizzkidd has just received his first ever pay-check (for just over $2,000) and decides to open a checking account with Megabank. On August 1, he pays the money into the account. He also arranges for some major recurring items of expenditure to be deducted regularly from his account by direct debit. He decides to keep a computerized record of his transactions.

● In the **Formula.xls** workbook, right-click on the **Sheet2** tab and choose the **Rename** command. Rename the sheet **Bankaccount**.

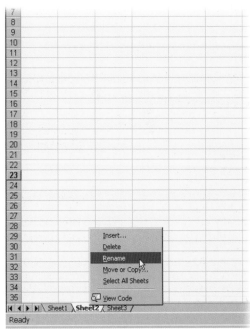

8 ❾ **Worksheet Tabs**

● In this example, we have decided on a set of very basic headings, which will apply in many cases. Enter the text labels and numbers shown below. You should widen the columns B to E and G to allow everything to fit comfortably.

	A	B	C	D	E	F	G	H
1	WIZZKIDD ACCOUNT AT MEGABANK							
2								
3	Date	Item	Income	Expenditure	Balance		Recurring items	
4	1-Aug	Paycheck					Paycheck	2128
5	4-Aug	Rent					Rent	921
6	20-Aug	Phone bill					Phone bill	55
7	1-Sep	Paycheck						
8	4-Sep	Rent						
9	20-Sep	Phone bill						

● Make a few formatting changes, using the formatting toolbar. Give the heading a larger type size, make it bold , and give it a color . Select row 3 and make it bold. Align column A left and align cells C3 to E3 right .

N33	▼	=						
	A	B	C	D	E	F	G	H
1	**WIZZKIDD ACCOUNT AT MEGABANK**							
2								
3	**Date**	**Item**	**Income**	**Expenditure**	**Balance**		**Recurring items**	
4	1-Aug	Paycheck					Paycheck	2128
5	4-Aug	Rent					Rent	921
6	20-Aug	Phone bill					Phone bill	55

● Select column B (by clicking on its header button). Then choose **Cells** from the **Format** menu, and in the **Format Cells** dialog box, click on the **Alignment** tab and check the **Wrap text** box. Click OK. Text that you enter into cells in column B will now "wrap" onto 2 lines if it goes over-length.

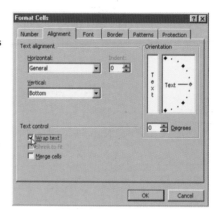

 ❷❺ **Bold**   ❹❶ **Font Color**   ❷❽ **Align Left**   ❸⓿ **Align Right**

● You now need to place all the recurring items of both income (for example, paycheck) and expenditure into the transaction register.

● To place the income items, click on cell C4, type an =, click on H4, and press Enter←. Then click on cell C7 and repeat the procedure.

	A	B	C	D	E	F	G	H
1	**WIZZKIDD ACCOUNT AT MEGABANK**							
2								
3	Date	Item	Income	Expenditure	Balance		Recurring items	
4	1-Aug	Paycheck	=H4				Paycheck	2128
5	4-Aug	Rent					Rent	921
6	20-Aug	Phone bill					Phone bill	55
7	1-Sep	Paycheck						
8	4-Sep	Rent						
9	20-Sep	Phone bill						
10								
11								

● Now we need to follow a similar procedure for the recurring expenditure items – the apartment rental and phone bill.

● In cells D5 and D8, enter the formula =H5. In cells D6 and D9, enter the formula =H6.

IF	▼ X ✓ =	=H6						
	A	B	C	D	E	F	G	H
1	**WIZZKIDD ACCOUNT AT MEGABANK**							
2								
3	Date	Item	Income	Expenditure	Balance		Recurring items	
4	1-Aug	Paycheck	2128				Paycheck	2128
5	4-Aug	Rent		921			Rent	921
6	20-Aug	Phone bill		=H6			Phone bill	55
7	1-Sep	Paycheck	2128					
8	4-Sep	Rent		921				
9	20-Sep	Phone bill						
10								

● Enter the opening balance (**2128**) in cell E4. The transaction register should now appear as shown at right.

	A	B	C	D	E
1	**WIZZKIDD ACCOUNT AT MEGABANK**				
2					
3	Date	Item	Income	Expenditure	Balance
4	1-Aug	Paycheck	2128		2128
5	4-Aug	Rent		921	
6	20-Aug	Phone bill		55	
7	1-Sep	Paycheck	2128		
8	4-Sep	Rent		921	
9	20-Sep	Phone bill		55	

● Highlight columns C to H and click the **Currency Style** ($) button on the formatting toolbar ⌐.

2 PROJECTING THE BALANCE

● In column E of the worksheet, Joe would like to see how his account balance changes with each item of income and expenditure, just as you see on a real bank statement.

● Select cell E5 and enter into it the formula =**E4+C5-D5**. This tells Excel to take the current balance ($2,128 in cell E4), add to it any income on this date (in cell C5 – none in this case) and then subtract any expenditure on this date (in cell D5 – $921 in this case) to give the new balance.

	IF	▼ × ✓ =	=E4+C5-D5					
	A	B	C	D	E	F	G	H
1	**WIZZKIDD ACCOUNT AT MEGABANK**							
2								
3	**Date**	**Item**	**Income**	**Expenditure**	**Balance**		**Recurring items**	
4	1-Aug	Paycheck	$ 2,128.00		$ 2,128.00		Paycheck	$2,128.00
5	4-Aug	Rent		$ 921.00	=E4+C5-D5		Rent	$ 921.00
6	20-Aug	Phone bill		$ 55.00			Phone bill	$ 55.00
7	1-Sep	Paycheck	$ 2,128.00					
8	4-Sep	Rent		$ 921.00				
9	20-Sep	Phone bill		$ 55.00				
10								

● Press [Enter↵]. Because of the $921 rental payment, Joe's balance has shrunk to $1,207. Now you are going to copy the formula in cell E5 into the rest of the **Balance** column. Select cell E5 again, and place the mouse pointer over the fill handle so that it turns into a small cross.

	E5	▼	=	=E4+C5-D5	
	A	B	C	D	E
1	**WIZZKIDD ACCOUNT AT MEGABANK**				
2					
3	**Date**	**Item**	**Income**	**Expenditure**	**Balance**
4	1-Aug	Paycheck	$ 2,128.00		$ 2,128.00
5	4-Aug	Rent		$ 921.00	$ 1,207.00
6	20-Aug	Phone bill		$ 55.00	
7	1-Sep	Paycheck	$ 2,128.00		
8	4-Sep	Rent		$ 921.00	
9	20-Sep	Phone bill		$ 55.00	
10					

❸❷ **Currency Style**

● Press down on the mouse button and drag downward, until the mouse pointer is positioned at the bottom right corner of cell E9, and the whole range E5:E9 is outlined.

	A	B	C	D	E
1	WIZZKIDD ACCOUNT AT MEGABANK				
2					
3	Date	Item	Income	Expenditure	Balance
4	1-Aug	Paycheck	$ 2,128.00		$ 2,128.00
5	4-Aug	Rent		$ 921.00	$ 1,207.00
6	20-Aug	Phone bill		$ 55.00	
7	1-Sep	Paycheck	$ 2,128.00		
8	4-Sep	Rent		$ 921.00	
9	20-Sep	Phone bill		$ 55.00	
10					

● Release the mouse button and the **Balance** column fills with the correct running balance figures – in each row, any income has been added, and expenditure subtracted, from the balance left after the previous transaction.

	A	B	C	D	E
1	WIZZKIDD ACCOUNT AT MEGABANK				
2					
3	Date	Item	Income	Expenditure	Balance
4	1-Aug	Paycheck	$ 2,128.00		$ 2,128.00
5	4-Aug	Rent		$ 921.00	$ 1,207.00
6	20-Aug	Phone bill		$ 55.00	$ 1,152.00
7	1-Sep	Paycheck	$ 2,128.00		$ 3,280.00
8	4-Sep	Rent		$ 921.00	$ 2,359.00
9	20-Sep	Phone bill		$ 55.00	$ 2,304.00
10					

● To see how Excel has achieved this feat, double-click on cell E5, look to see what it contains, and then repeat for cells E6, E7, etc.

● You will see that when it copied the formula in E5 into the subsequent cells, Excel adjusted the formula in each case. For example, cell E6 contains the formula (=**E5+C6-D6**). In each case, the cell contains a formula that adds any income and subtracts any expenditure in its own row to the previous balance, so giving the correct running balance figures.

● To understand how these formulas came to be created, see the box feature on relative and absolute cell references ⌐.

IF	▼	× √ =	=E5+C6-D6				
	A	B	C	D	E	F	G	H
1	WIZZKIDD ACCOUNT AT MEGABANK						
2							
3	Date	Item	Income	Expenditure	Balance		Recurring items	
4	1-Aug	Paycheck	$ 2,128.00		$ 2,128.00		Paycheck	$2,128.00
5	4-Aug	Rent		$ 921.00	$ 1,207.00		Rent	$ 921.00
6	20-Aug	Phone bill		$ 55.00	=E5+C6-D6		Phone bill	$ 55.00
7	1-Sep	Paycheck	$ 2,128.00		$ 3,280.00			
8	4-Sep	Rent		$ 921.00	$ 2,359.00			
9	20-Sep	Phone bill		$ 55.00	$ 2,304.00			

26 **Relative and Absolute Cell References**

RELATIVE AND ABSOLUTE CELL REFERENCES

In Excel, two different types of cell references can be used in formulas. They are called relative and absolute cell references, and it is very important to understand the differences between the two different types of references.

RELATIVE CELL REFERENCES.

● Relative references are the default type, and locate the position of other cells relative to the position of the cell containing the formula. For example, the cell reference B6 within a formula in cell D6 means "the value of the cell two cells to the left of this one." So the formula "=D5+B6" in cell D6 would mean "take the value in the cell above this one, and add the value in the cell two cells to the left of this one."

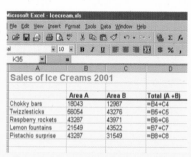

Worksheet displaying formulas in column D

● When a formula containing relative cell references is copied to other cells, the cell references are updated accordingly. This usually gives the desired result when the copied formulas are used to combine two or more series of data in a repetitive way. For example, in the worksheet shown at the right, each cell in the **Total (A +B)** column contains a formula that adds together the values of the two cells to its left. This was achieved by copying the formula "=B4+C4" in cell D4 downward into the cells below it.

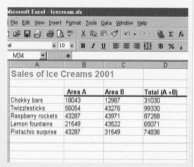

Worksheet displaying values in column D

THE #REF! ERROR

If you delete or clear a cell that is referenced by a formula elsewhere, then a #REF! error appears in the cell containing the formula. The error occurs because the cell contents that had been referenced no longer exist. In such instances, you must either restore the cleared or deleted cell, or fix the formula that referenced it.

RELATIVE AND ABSOLUTE CELL REFERENCES (CONT.)

ABSOLUTE CELL REFERENCES

● An absolute cell reference is needed when you want the reference always to "point" to a particular worksheet cell, no matter where the formula containing the reference is copied to. Absolute cell references are distinguished by having $ signs placed in front of the column and row identifiers (for example, $B$3 instead of B3).

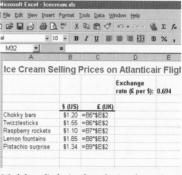

Worksheet displaying formulas in column C

● In the worksheets shown at the right, the cells in the range C5:C9 contain formulas that calculate the £ sterling equivalents of the US dollar amounts in column B. The formula in each cell multiplies the US dollar figure in the cell to its left by the exchange rate figure held in cell E2, using the absolute cell reference $E$2.

● Absolute cell references do not change when they are copied to other cells. The figures in column C at right were achieved by putting the formula "=B5*$E$2" in cell C5 and then copying this formula downward.

Worksheet displaying values in column C

MIXED CELL REFERENCES

It is possible to have a mixed cell reference, partly relative and partly absolute, for example, $C8 or C$12. When formulas containing such references are copied, they will adjust in one direction (i.e., along a row or down a column), but not in the other direction. Although Excel experts often use them, mixed cell references can be confusing and are best avoided by beginners.

3 ADDING NEW TRANSACTIONS

● Adding new transactions into the account ledger is easy.

You need to insert extra rows, add the new transactions (or the intended transactions), then recopy the formula

that calculates the running balance. Try the following:
● Select row 7 and choose **Rows** from the **Insert** menu.

● Add the text and figures shown at right into row 7 (**23-Aug/Cash withdrawal/ 350**). Just type **350** into cell D7 – the $ sign will be added automatically.

● Insert another blank row in row 8 and add the income item **29 Aug/Check from Grandma/60** as shown at right. In row 12, add the intended expenditure item **22 Sep/Vacation in Bermuda/2200**.

	A	B	C	D	E
1	WIZZKIDD ACCOUNT AT MEGABANK				
2					
3	Date	Item	Income	Expenditure	Balance
4	1-Aug	Paycheck	$ 2,128.00		$ 2,128.00
5	4-Aug	Rent		$ 921.00	$ 1,207.00
6	20-Aug	Phone bill		$ 55.00	$ 1,152.00
7	23-Aug	Cash withdrawal		$ 350.00	
8	29-Aug	Check from Grandma	$ 60.00		
9	1-Sep	Paycheck	$ 2,128.00		$ 3,280.00
10	4-Sep	Rent		$ 921.00	$ 2,359.00
11	20-Sep	Phone bill		$ 55.00	$ 2,304.00
12	22-Sep	Vacation in Bermuda		$ 2,200.00	
13					

● Now select cell E6, and drag its fill handle downward to copy the formula it contains to E12, in order to display the new running balance information.

1	WIZZKIDD ACCOUNT AT MEGABANK				
2					
3	Date	Item	Income	Expenditure	Balance
4	1-Aug	Paycheck	$ 2,128.00		$ 2,128.00
5	4-Aug	Rent		$ 921.00	$ 1,207.00
6	20-Aug	Phone bill		$ 55.00	$ 1,152.00
7	23-Aug	Cash withdrawal		$ 350.00	
8	29-Aug	Check from Grandma	$ 60.00		
9	1-Sep	Paycheck	$ 2,128.00		$ 3,280.00
10	4-Sep	Rent		$ 921.00	$ 2,359.00
11	20-Sep	Phone bill		$ 55.00	$ 2,304.00
12	22-Sep	Vacation in Bermuda		$ 2,200.00	
13					

● The display shows Joe that his account will go overdrawn on September 22 if he goes ahead with his intended vacation. He decides to "downsize" his vacation aspirations – and do something else with his hard-earned cash. Delete row 12 from the worksheet and then save the workbook.

1	WIZZKIDD ACCOUNT AT MEGABANK				
2					
3	Date	Item	Income	Expenditure	Balance
4	1-Aug	Paycheck	$ 2,128.00		$ 2,128.00
5	4-Aug	Rent		$ 921.00	$ 1,207.00
6	20-Aug	Phone bill		$ 55.00	$ 1,152.00
7	23-Aug	Cash withdrawal		$ 350.00	$ 802.00
8	29-Aug	Check from Grandma	$ 60.00		$ 862.00
9	1-Sep	Paycheck	$ 2,128.00		$ 2,990.00
10	4-Sep	Rent		$ 921.00	$ 2,069.00
11	20-Sep	Phone bill		$ 55.00	$ 2,014.00
12	22-Sep	Vacation in Bermuda		$ 2,200.00	$ (186.00)

EXTENDING FORMULAS

This chapter looks at some further applications of formulas,
such as their use in linking data between different worksheets,
as applied to the bank balance projection you have created.

USING ABSOLUTE CELL REFERENCES

In the box on relative and absolute cell references (on page 27), you learned that you should always use absolute cell references in a formula when you want the references to "point" to the same cells in the worksheet, wherever the formula is copied. Let's try putting some absolute cell references into practice.

1 CONVERTING CELL REFERENCES
● Click on cell C4, then on D5 and then D6 in the **Bankaccount** worksheet. Look in the formula bar each time. These cells contain relative cell references that "point" to the master data about recurring items of income and expenditure held in cells H4, H5, and H6. If the cell references were changed from relative to absolute, their data could be copied to subsequent months in the bank account projection and would still "point" to the same master data. So, let's change them from relative to absolute.

	C4	▼	= =H4				
	A	B	C	D	E	F	G	H
1	WIZZKIDD ACCOUNT AT MEGABANK							
2								
3	Date	Item	Income	Expenditure	Balance		Recurring items	
4	1-Aug	Paycheck	$ 2,128.00		$ 2,128.00		Paycheck	$ 2,128.00
5	4-Aug	Rent		$ 921.00	$ 1,207.00		Rent	$ 921.00
6	20-Aug	Phone bill		$ 55.00	$ 1,152.00		Phone bill	$ 55.00
7	23-Aug	Cash withdrawal		$ 350.00	$ 802.00			
8	29-Aug	Check from Grandma	$ 60.00		$ 862.00			
9	1-Sep	Paycheck	$ 2,128.00		$ 2,990.00			
10	4-Sep	Rent		$ 921.00	$ 2,069.00			
11	20-Sep	Phone bill		$ 55.00	$ 2,014.00			
12								

● Click again on cell C4, and then in the formula bar, click on the relative cell reference H4.

	IF	▼	× ✓ =	=H4	
	A	B	C	D	E
1	WIZZKIDD ACCOUNT AT MEGABANK				
2					
3	Date	Item	Income	Expenditure	Balance
4	1-Aug	Paycheck	=H4		$ 2,128.00
5	4-Aug	Rent		$ 921.00	$ 1,207.00
6	20-Aug	Phone bill		$ 55.00	$ 1,152.00

● Press the F4 key and the relative reference changes to an absolute reference ($H$4). Press Enter ↲.

	A	B	C	D	E
1	WIZZKIDD ACCOUNT AT MEGABANK				
2					
3	Date	Item	Income	Expenditure	Balance
4	1-Aug	Paycheck	=$H$4		$ 2,128.00
5	4-Aug	Rent		$ 921.00	$ 1,207.00
6	20-Aug	Phone bill		$ 55.00	$ 1,152.00

● Now change the relative cell references in cells D5 and D6 to absolute references (from =H5 to =$H$5 and from =H6 to =$H$6 respectively).

	A	B	C	D	E
1	WIZZKIDD ACCOUNT AT MEGABANK				
2					
3	Date	Item	Income	Expenditure	Balance
4	1-Aug	Paycheck	$ 2,128.00		$ 2,128.00
5	4-Aug	Rent		$ 921.00	$ 1,207.00
6	20-Aug	Phone bill		=$H$6	$ 1,152.00
7	23-Aug	Cash withdrawal		$ 350.00	$ 802.00
		Check from			

2 COPYING THE DATA

● You can now copy the data concerning recurring items of income and expenditure to future months in the checking account transaction register.

● Select the whole range B4 to D6 and then click on the **Copy** button.

	Microsoft Excel - Formula.xls				
	File Edit View Insert Format Tools Data Window Help				
	🗋 🖆 🖫 🖨 🖨 🔍 ✂ 💾 🛍 ✍ ⟳ ▾ ⟲ ▾ 🔵 Σ ƒ				
	Arial	▾ 10 ▾	**B** ▾Copy	📰 📰 🗐 $ % ,	
	B4	▼	= Paycheck		
	A	B	C	D	E
1	WIZZKIDD ACCOUNT AT MEGABANK				
2					
3	Date	Item	Income	Expenditure	Balance
4	1-Aug	Paycheck	$ 2,128.00		$ 2,128.00
5	4-Aug	Rent		$ 921.00	$ 1,207.00
6	20-Aug	Phone bill		$ 55.00	$ 1,152.00
7	23-Aug	Cash withdrawal		$ 350.00	$ 802.00
		Check from			

● Select cell B9 and then click on the **Paste** button.

● Now select cell B12 and click on the **Paste** button again. Select cell B15 and repeat one more time.

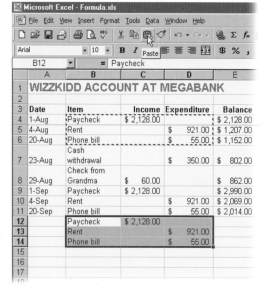

● In cells A12 to A17, fill in the October and November dates for the recurring transactions, as shown at right.

11	20-Sep	Phone bill		$	55.00	$ 2,014.00
12	1-Oct	Paycheck	$ 2,128.00			
13	4-Oct	Rent		$	921.00	
14	20-Oct	Phone bill		$	55.00	
15	1-Nov	Paycheck	$ 2,128.00			
16	4-Nov	Rent		$	921.00	
17	20-Nov	Phone bill		$	55.00	
18						

● Now copy down the running balance formula from cell E11 to E17, by dragging the fill handle. Save your workbook.

9	1-Sep	Paycheck	$ 2,128.00			$ 2,990.00
10	4-Sep	Rent		$	921.00	$ 2,069.00
11	20-Sep	Phone bill		$	55.00	$ 2,014.00
12	1-Oct	Paycheck	$ 2,128.00			
13	4-Oct	Rent		$	921.00	
14	20-Oct	Phone bill		$	55.00	
15	1-Nov	Paycheck	$ 2,128.00			
16	4-Nov	Rent		$	921.00	
17	20-Nov	Phone bill		$	55.00	
18						

LINKING WORKSHEETS

As well as in the worksheet itself, cell references in formulas can refer to data in other worksheets or even in other workbooks. This means that formulas can be used to link data in different worksheets. This is a powerful tool because it allows selected data from a number of source worksheets (perhaps dealing with different aspects of a business or home finances) to be collected into a summary or more general dependent worksheet, for example, a business sales summary or a bank balance projection. Then, if any of the source data changes in the future, the data in the dependent worksheet will automatically update. In this example, we'll set up a worksheet dealing with some of Joe Wizzkidd's stock investments and link this in to his bank balance projection.

1 THE INVESTMENT WORKSHEET
● In your **Formulas.xls** worksheet, rename **Sheet 3** as **Stock Portfolio**.

28	
29	Insert...
30	Delete
31	Rename
32	Move or Copy...
33	Select All Sheets
34	
35	View Code

|◄ ◄ ► ►|\ Sheet1 / Bankaccount \Sheet3 /

● As was the case with the Bank Balance projection , basic headings have been compiled. Enter the data that is shown below. The costs of the investments and dividends per stock unit are Joe's estimates or forecasts at this stage.

	A	B	C	D	E	F	G	H	I
1	Wizzkid's Stock Portfolio								
2									
3	Date bought	Stock	Stock units	Cost	Dividend date	Dividend per stock unit (cents)	Total dividend (dollars)		
4	10-Sep-02	Fantasy Ices Corp	110	865	22-Oct-02	33			
5	10-Sep-02	MegaPharm	88	1154	24-Oct-02	25			
6									
7									

● Now add some formatting. Enlarge the heading and give it a color. Select row 3, make it bold and wrap the text in it (see page 22). Select column D and then click on the **Currency Style** ($) button on the formatting toolbar; repeat with column G. Select cell D6, add a top and bottom border to it (use the **Borders** button on the formatting toolbar), then enter the formula =**D4+D5** into it and press Enter. Cell D6 now contains the total estimated cost of Joe's investments.

Microsoft Excel - Formulas.xls

File Edit View Insert Format Tools Data Window Help

Arial 10 B I U $ % ,

SUM =D4+D5

	A	B	C	D	E
1	Wizzkid's Stock Portfolio				
2					
3	Date bought	Stock	Stock units	Cost	Dividend date
4	10-Sep-02	Fantasy Ices Corp	110	$ 865.00	22-Oct-02
5	10-Sep-02	MegaPharm	88	$1,154.00	24-Oct-02
6				=D4+D5	
7					

● To estimate the October dividend from Fantasy Ices Corp, you need to multiply the number of stock units by the estimated dividend, then divide by 100 to convert cents to dollars. So, enter =**C4*F4/100** in cell G4.

	Stock units	Cost	Dividend date	Dividend per stock unit (cents)	Total dividend (dollars)
Ices Corp	110	$ 865.00	22-Oct-02	33	=C4*F4/100
arm	88	$1,154.00	24-Oct-02	25	
		$2,019.00			

21 A Bank Balance Projection

32 Currency Style

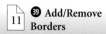
39 Add/Remove Borders

- Copy the formula in cell G4 to G5 (using the fill handle) to give the estimated dividend from MegaPharm.

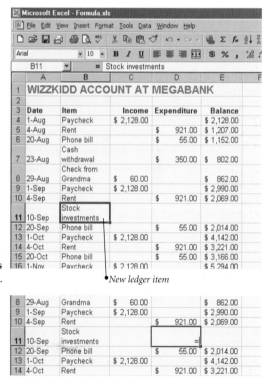

B	C	D	E	F	G
tock Portfolio					
ck	Stock units	Cost	Dividend date	Dividend per stock unit (cents)	Total dividend (dollars)
tasy Ices Corp	110	$ 865.00	22-Oct-02	33	$ 36.30
gaPharm	88	$1,154.00	24-Oct-02	25	
		$2,019.00			

2 ESTABLISHING A LINK

- You are now going to make some links between Joe's **Stock Portfolio** worksheet and his bank account worksheet. The two main ways of creating links between worksheets, are by "pointing," and by using the **Paste Special** command. Let's try "pointing" first.

- Reopen the **Bank-account** worksheet (by clicking its tab at the foot of the Excel window). Insert a new row at row 11 and type **10-Sep** into cell A11 and **Stock investments** into cell B11. Press Enter↵.

Microsoft Excel - Formula.xls

File Edit View Insert Format Tools Data Window Help

Arial 10 B I U $ % ‚ .0

B11 Stock investments

	A	B	C	D	E	F
1	WIZZKIDD ACCOUNT AT MEGABANK					
2						
3	Date	Item	Income	Expenditure	Balance	
4	1-Aug	Paycheck	$ 2,128.00		$ 2,128.00	
5	4-Aug	Rent		$ 921.00	$ 1,207.00	
6	20-Aug	Phone bill		$ 55.00	$ 1,152.00	
7	23-Aug	Cash withdrawal		$ 350.00	$ 802.00	
8	29-Aug	Check from Grandma	$ 60.00		$ 862.00	
9	1-Sep	Paycheck	$ 2,128.00		$ 2,990.00	
10	4-Sep	Rent		$ 921.00	$ 2,069.00	
11	10-Sep	Stock investments				
12	20-Sep	Phone bill		$ 55.00	$ 2,014.00	
13	1-Oct	Paycheck	$ 2,128.00		$ 4,142.00	
14	4-Oct	Rent		$ 921.00	$ 3,221.00	
15	20-Oct	Phone bill		$ 55.00	$ 3,166.00	
16	1-Nov	Paycheck	$ 2,128.00		$ 5,294.00	

New ledger item

- Select cell D11 and type an = (equals) sign.

8	29-Aug	Grandma	$ 60.00		$ 862.00
9	1-Sep	Paycheck	$ 2,128.00		$ 2,990.00
10	4-Sep	Rent		$ 921.00	$ 2,069.00
11	10-Sep	Stock investments		=	
12	20-Sep	Phone bill		$ 55.00	$ 2,014.00
13	1-Oct	Paycheck	$ 2,128.00		$ 4,142.00
14	4-Oct	Rent		$ 921.00	$ 3,221.00

● Now switch to the **StockPortfolio** worksheet and click on cell D6, which contains the total cost of the stock investments. Press Enter ↵.

	A	B	C	D	E
1	**Wizzkid's Stock Portfolio**				
2					
3	**Date bought**	**Stock**	**Stock units**	**Cost**	**Dividend date**
4	10-Sep-02	Fantasy Ices Corp	110	$ 865.00	22-Oct-02
5	10-Sep-02	MegaPharm	88	$1,154.00	24-Oct-02
6				$2,019.00	
7					

● You will automatically be switched back to the **Bankaccount** worksheet, where cell D11 now contains the total cost of the stock investments (**$2,019.00**). The active cell is now the cell below.

10	4-Sep	Rent		$	921.00	$ 2,069.00
11	10-Sep	Stock investments		$	2,019.00	
12	20-Sep	Phone bill		$	55.00	$ 2,014.00
13	1-Oct	Paycheck	$ 2,128.00			$ 4,142.00
14	4-Oct	Rent		$	921.00	$ 3,221.00
15	20-Oct	Phone bill		$	55.00	$ 3,166.00
16	1-Nov	Paycheck	$ 2,128.00			$ 5,294.00
17	4-Nov	Rent		$	921.00	$ 4,373.00

● Click on cell D11 and look in the formula bar. It contains the formula: ='Stock Portfolio'!D6. The expression "'Stock Portfolio'!D6" is an external reference to cell D6 in the **StockPortfolio** worksheet.

Microsoft Excel - Formulas.xls

File Edit View Insert Format Tools Data Window Help

Arial ... 10 ... B I U 象 象 象 國 $ % ,

D11 ... = ='Stock Portfolio'!D6

	A	B	C	D	E
1	WIZZKIDD ACCOUNT AT MEGABANK				

External reference ●

3 USING PASTE SPECIAL

● Now let's link the dividend payments into the **Bankaccount** worksheet.

● In the **Bankaccount** worksheet, add two more rows after row 15, and enter the data in cells A16, A17, B16, and B17 shown at the right.

12	20-Sep	Phone bill		$	55.00	$ 2,014.00
13	1-Oct	Paycheck	$ 2,128.00			$ 4,142.00
14	4-Oct	Rent		$	921.00	$ 3,221.00
15	20-Oct	Phone bill		$	55.00	$ 3,166.00
16	22-Oct	Fantasy Ices dividend				
17	24-Oct	MegaPharm dividend				
18	1-Nov	Paycheck	$ 2,128.00			$ 5,294.00
19	4-Nov	Rent		$	921.00	$ 4,373.00
20	20-Nov	Phone bill		$	55.00	$ 4,318.00
21						
22						

● Now switch to the **Stock-Portfolio** sheet, click on cell G4 (the estimated Fantasy Ices dividend) and click the **Copy** button on the formatting toolbar.

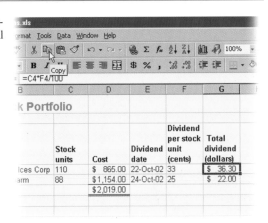

● Switch back to the **Bankaccount** sheet and select cell C16, where you want to enter the linked data. Choose **Paste Special** from the **Edit** menu.

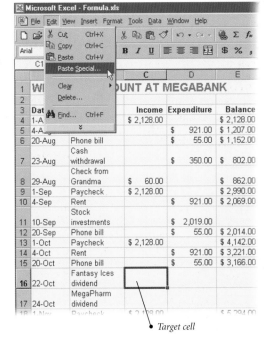

Target cell

● In the **Paste Special** dialog box, click on the **Paste Link** button. This links the Fantasy Ices dividend data into cell C16 of the **Bankaccount** worksheet.

● Return to the **Stock-Portfolio** sheet and repeat these three steps to link the MegaPharm dividend data (cell G5) into the **Bank-account** sheet at cell C17.

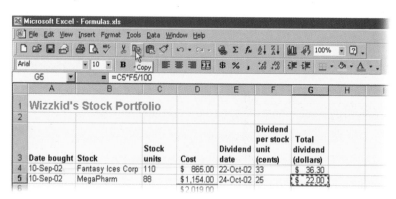

	A	B	C	D	E	F	G	H	I
1	**Wizzkid's Stock Portfolio**								
2									
3	Date bought	Stock	Stock units	Cost	Dividend date	Dividend per stock unit (cents)	Total dividend (dollars)		
4	10-Sep-02	Fantasy Ices Corp	110	$ 865.00	22-Oct-02	33	$ 36.30		
5	10-Sep-02	MegaPharm	88	$1,154.00	24-Oct-02	25	$ 22.00		
6				$2,019.00					

DECIDING BETWEEN PASTE SPECIAL AND POINTING

There is an important difference between the links forged using the **Paste Special** command and those made by the pointing method. In those made using the **Paste Special** command, the external references are absolute cell references, whereas those forged by pointing are relative cell references. If the cells containing linked data created by pointing are copied, they will point to different cells in the source data sheet.

● Both dividends are now linked into the **Bankaccount** worksheet. Recalculate the running balance by copying the formula in E10 all the way down to E20 (by selecting E10 and then dragging the fill handle).

	Check from			
Aug	Grandma	$ 60.00		$ 862.00
ep	Paycheck	$ 2,128.00		$ 2,990.00
ep	Rent		$ 921.00	$ 2,069.00
Sep	Stock investments		$ 2,019.00	
Sep	Phone bill		$ 55.00	$ 2,014.00
ct	Paycheck	$ 2,128.00		$ 4,142.00
ct	Rent		$ 921.00	$ 3,221.00
Oct	Phone bill		$ 55.00	$ 3,166.00
Oct	Fantasy Ices dividend	$ 36.30		
Oct	MegaPharm dividend	$ 22.00		
ov	Paycheck	$ 2,128.00		$ 5,294.00
ov	Rent		$ 921.00	$ 4,373.00
Nov	Phone bill		$ 55.00	$ 4,318.00

4 ALTERING THE SOURCE DATA

● Now see what happens when you alter the linked source data.

● Switch back to the **StockPortfolio** sheet and change the value in cell D4 to **$875** (the brokerage costs were slightly higher than Joe first thought). When you make the change, you will see that the value in cell D6 also updates.

● Alter the amounts in cells F4 and F5 to **35** and **26** respectively (both companies paid out higher dividends per stock unit than expected). Note that the values in G4 and G5 also update.

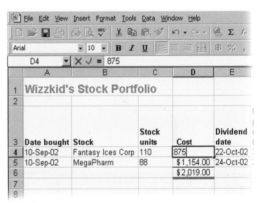

File Edit View Insert Format Tools Data Window Help

Arial 10 B I U $ %

D4 = 875

Wizzkid's Stock Portfolio

	A	B	C	D	E
1	Wizzkid's Stock Portfolio				
2					
3	Date bought	Stock	Stock units	Cost	Dividend date
4	10-Sep-02	Fantasy Ices Corp	110	875	22-Oct-02
5	10-Sep-02	MegaPharm	88	$1,154.00	24-Oct-02
6				$2,019.00	
7					
8					

ock Portfolio

	B	C	D	E	F	G
	.k	Stock units	Cost	Dividend date	Dividend per stock unit (cents)	Total dividend (dollars)
	asy Ices Corp	110	$ 875.00	22-Oct-02	35	$ 38.50
	Pharm	88	$1,154.00	24-Oct-02	26	$ 22.00
			$2,029.00			

● Switch back to the **Bankaccount** worksheet and note that the figures in D11 and in C16 and C17, which all rely on the altered data in the **StockPortfolio** worksheet, have all been automatically updated. Also, all the running balance figures from row 10 downward have been altered.

● Joe notes with dismay that his account is projected to be overdrawn by September 20.

	A	B	C	D	E
1	WIZZKIDD ACCOUNT AT MEGABANK				
2					
3	Date	Item	Income	Expenditure	Balance
4	1-Aug	Paycheck	$ 2,128.00		$ 2,128.00
5	4-Aug	Rent		$ 921.00	$ 1,207.00
6	20-Aug	Phone bill		$ 55.00	$ 1,152.00
7	23-Aug	Cash withdrawal		$ 350.00	$ 802.00
8	29-Aug	Check from Grandma	$ 60.00		$ 862.00
9	1-Sep	Paycheck	$ 2,128.00		$ 2,990.00
10	4-Sep	Rent		$ 921.00	$ 2,069.00
11	10-Sep	Stock investments		$ 2,029.00	$ 40.00
12	20-Sep	Phone bill		$ 55.00	$ (15.00)
13	1-Oct	Paycheck	$ 2,128.00		$ 2,113.00
14	4-Oct	Rent		$ 921.00	$ 1,192.00
15	20-Oct	Phone bill		$ 55.00	$ 1,137.00
16	22-Oct	Fantasy Ices dividend	$ 38.50		$ 1,175.50
17	24-Oct	MegaPharm dividend	$ 22.88		$ 1,198.38
18	1-Nov	Paycheck	$ 2,128.00		$ 3,326.38
19	4-Nov	Rent		$ 921.00	$ 2,405.38
20	20-Nov	Phone bill		$ 55.00	$ 2,350.38

Projected overdraft ●

5 AVOIDING AN OVERDRAFT

● Megabank will charge $50 if his account becomes overdrawn, even if it is for a small amount for a few days! Joe realizes that he can avoid the problem by borrowing $20 from a friend, depositing the cash into the bank, and paying the friend back with interest a couple of weeks later.

● Enter new blank rows in the **Bankaccount** worksheet for the dates Sep 18 and Oct 2 and add the entries shown in rows 12 and 15 shown at right.

	A	B	C	D	E
1	WIZZKIDD ACCOUNT AT MEGABANK				
2					
3	Date	Item	Income	Expenditure	Balance
4	1-Aug	Paycheck	$ 2,128.00		$ 2,128.00
5	4-Aug	Rent		$ 921.00	$ 1,207.00
6	20-Aug	Phone bill		$ 55.00	$ 1,152.00
7	23-Aug	Cash withdrawal		$ 350.00	$ 802.00
8	29-Aug	Check from Grandma	$ 60.00		$ 862.00
9	1-Sep	Paycheck	$ 2,128.00		$ 2,990.00
10	4-Sep	Rent		$ 921.00	$ 2,069.00
11	10-Sep	Stock investments		$ 2,029.00	$ 40.00
12	18-Sep	Cash from Steve	$ 20.00		
13	20-Sep	Phone bill		$ 55.00	$ (15.00)
14	1-Oct	Paycheck	$ 2,128.00		$ 2,113.00
15	2-Oct	Cash for Steve		$ 21.00	
16	4-Oct	Rent		$ 921.00	$ 1,192.00
17	20-Oct	Phone bill		$ 55.00	$ 1,137.00
		Fantasy Ices			

● Reproject the running balance from cell E11 downward to cell E22.

8	29-Aug	Grandma	$ 60.00			$ 862.00
9	1-Sep	Paycheck	$ 2,128.00			$ 2,990.00
10	4-Sep	Rent			$ 921.00	$ 2,069.00
11	10-Sep	Stock investments			$ 2,029.00	$ 40.00
12	18-Sep	Cash from Steve	$ 20.00			
13	20-Sep	Phone bill			$ 55.00	$ (15.00)
14	1-Oct	Paycheck	$ 2,128.00			$ 2,113.00
15	2-Oct	Cash for Steve			$ 21.00	
16	4-Oct	Rent			$ 921.00	$ 1,192.00
17	20-Oct	Phone bill			$ 55.00	$ 1,137.00
18	22-Oct	Fantasy Ices dividend	$ 38.50			$ 1,175.50
19	24-Oct	MegaPharm dividend	$ 22.88			$ 1,198.38
20	1-Nov	Paycheck	$ 2,128.00			$ 3,326.38
21	4-Nov	Rent			$ 921.00	$ 2,405.38
22	20-Nov	Phone bill			$ 55.00	$ 2,350.38
23						
24						
25						

● The overdraft charge is now avoided, since the running balance never falls below zero. Joe has saved himself $49.

8	29-Aug	Grandma	$ 60.00			$ 862.00
9	1-Sep	Paycheck	$ 2,128.00			$ 2,990.00
10	4-Sep	Rent			$ 921.00	$ 2,069.00
11	10-Sep	Stock investments			$ 2,029.00	$ 40.00
12	18-Sep	Cash from Steve	$ 20.00			$ 60.00
13	20-Sep	Phone bill			$ 55.00	$ 5.00
14	1-Oct	Paycheck	$ 2,128.00			$ 2,133.00
15	2-Oct	Cash for Steve			$ 21.00	$ 2,112.00
16	4-Oct	Rent			$ 921.00	$ 1,191.00
17	20-Oct	Phone bill			$ 55.00	$ 1,136.00
18	22-Oct	Fantasy Ices dividend	$ 38.50			$ 1,174.50
19	24-Oct	MegaPharm dividend	$ 22.88			$ 1,197.38
20	1-Nov	Paycheck	$ 2,128.00			$ 3,325.38
21	4-Nov	Rent			$ 921.00	$ 2,404.38
22	20-Nov	Phone bill			$ 55.00	$ 2,349.38
23						

LINKING WORKBOOKS

Linking data from a worksheet in one workbook to one in another workbook is done in the same way as linking sheets in the same workbook. If data in the source workbook changes while the "target" workbook is closed, when the "target" workbook reopens, a message asks if you want to update all linked data.

FUNCTIONS

Excel formulas can be made to perform much more complex operations than you've seen so far. To help, Excel provides ready-made calculation tools called functions.

FUNCTION BASICS

Each function carries out a specific operation on some data, and each has a name. For example, the **SQRT** function finds the square root of a given number, and the **AVERAGE** function calculates the average (or mean) of a list of numbers. Functions can save you from having to type in complex formulas. However, you usually still have to provide the data on which the function will work. The data required by a function to perform its particular task may be the values in a particular cell or range of cells, or a number or a piece of text you provide. These pieces of data required by a function are called the function's arguments. Different functions vary in the number of arguments they require.

1 USING THE SUM FUNCTION

● In the **Formula.xls** workbook, choose **Worksheet** from the **Insert** menu to create a new worksheet. Name it **Functions** and enter the figures and text labels shown at the right.

	A	B	C	D	E
1	Science exam scores				
2					
3		Physics (%)	Biology (%)	Chemistry (%)	Average
4	Anne	98	72	95	
5	Bill	71	66	85	
6	Cheryl	58	75	63	
7	Dan	81	84	90	
8	Total				
9					
10					
11					
12					

Microsoft Excel - Formula.xls

File Edit View Insert Format Tools Data Window Help

Arial   10   B I U

M27   =

● In cell B8, you want the total of the Physics scores. You could enter the formula =B4+B5+B6+B7. But there's a quicker way, using the SUM function. So instead, type **=SUM(B4:B7)**. This means "add together the values in the range of cells B4 to B7." In this case, the cell values in the range B4:B7 are the SUM function's argument.

	A	B	C	D	E
1	Science exam scores				
2					
3		Physics (%)	Biology (%)	Chemistry (%)	Average
4	Anne	98	72	95	
5	Bill	71	66	85	
6	Cheryl	58	75	63	
7	Dan	81	84	90	
8	Total	=SUM(B4:B7)			

IF =SUM(B4:B7)

Microsoft Excel - Formula.xls
File Edit View Insert Format Tools Data Window Help

● Press [Enter ←] and the total of the Physics scores are displayed in cell B8.

B9 =

	A	B	C	D	E
1	Science exam scores				
2					
3		Physics (%)	Biology (%)	Chemistry (%)	Average
4	Anne	98	72	95	
5	Bill	71	66	85	
6	Cheryl	58	75	63	
7	Dan	81	84	90	
8	Total	308			
9					

2 COPYING A FUNCTION

● As with any other formula, a formula that contains a function can be copied to other cells. If the function's arguments contain relative cell references, then these will adjust appropriately during the copying process.
● Select cell B8 and then copy it to cell C8 by dragging its fill handle to the right.

Microsoft Excel - Formula.xls
File Edit View Insert Format Tools Data Window Help

Arial 10 B I U $ % ,

B8 =SUM(B4:B7)

	A	B	C	D	E
1	Science exam scores				
2					
3		Physics (%)	Biology (%)	Chemistry (%)	Average
4	Anne	98	72	95	
5	Bill	71	66	85	
6	Cheryl	58	75	63	
7	Dan	81	84	90	
8	Total	308			
9					
10					

● On completing the copy, cell C8 displays the figure **297** – the total of the Biology scores – just as you want.

	A	B	C	D	E
	B8	= =SUM(B4:B7)			
1	Science exam scores				
2					
3		Physics (%)	Biology (%)	Chemistry (%)	Averag
4	Anne	98	72	95	
5	Bill	71	66	85	
6	Cheryl	58	75	63	
7	Dan	81	84	90	
8	Total	308	297		
9					
10					

● Double-clicking on cell C8 shows that it contains the formula =**SUM(C4:C7)** – an appropriately adjusted version of the formula in cell B8.

	A	B	C	D	E
	IF	▾ X ✓ =	=SUM(C4:C7)		
1	Science exam scores				
2					
3		Physics (%)	Biology (%)	Chemistry (%)	Average
4	Anne	98	72	95	
5	Bill	71	66	85	
6	Cheryl	58	75	63	
7	Dan	81	84	90	
8	Total	308	=SUM(C4:C7)		
9					

3 THE AUTOSUM BUTTON

● The SUM function is such a commonly used one that Excel provides a special toolbar button to activate it.

● Select cell D8 and then click on the **AutoSum** button on the standard toolbar.

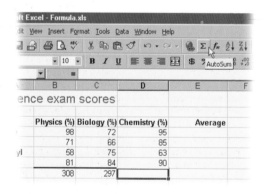

⑮ AutoSum

● The formula =SUM(D4:D7) is automatically inserted in cell D8 and a flashing border appears around the range **D4:D7**.

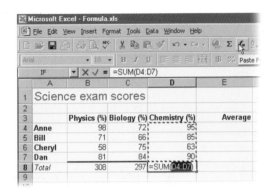

● Press Enter← to confirm that you want the sum of the cell values in the range **D4:D7** placed in cell D8. Now you have calculated the candidates' totals for all three of the science examinations.

	A	B	C	D	E
1	Science exam scores				
2					
3		Physics (%)	Biology (%)	Chemistry (%)	Average
4	Anne	98	72	95	
5	Bill	71	66	85	
6	Cheryl	58	75	63	
7	Dan	81	84	90	
8	Total	308	297	333	
9					
10					
11					

Function Syntax
The general form of an Excel function is "= FUNCTION (argument 1; argument 2; etc)" where FUNCTION is the name of the function, and argument 1, argument 2 etc. are the function's arguments.

THE AUTOSUM BUTTON

The **AutoSum** button works best if the selected cell (into which a sum is to be placed) is either the cell immediately to the right of a continuous row of cell values to be added, or immediately below a continuous column of cell values to be added. In both these instances, the appropriate cell values to be added are chosen when you click the **AutoSum** button. In other cases, you can choose the range of cell values to be added by dragging the mouse pointer across the range immediately after clicking the **AutoSum** button and before pressing Enter←

USING THE FUNCTION WIZARD

To facilitate the use of functions in worksheets, the Excel program provides assistance in the form of the **Paste Function** command (this is also called the Function Wizard), which takes you step-by-step through the process. Follow the steps below to use the **AVERAGE** function and then to try out a different statistical function, called the **CORREL** function.

1 FINDING AVERAGES

● In column E of the **Functions** worksheet, you want to put each candidate's average score for the three science exams.
● First, select cell E4 and then click on the **Paste Function** button (labeled *fx*).

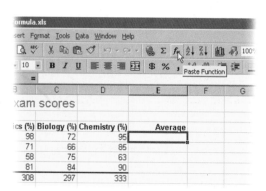

● The **Paste Function** dialog box appears. On the left-hand side, under **Function category**, click on **All**. On the right-hand side, scroll down until you see **AVERAGE** and click on this function to choose it. A description of what the function does appears at the foot of the dialog box. Finally, click on **OK**.

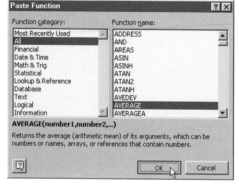

⑯ Paste Function

● A second, untitled, dialog box appears at the top-left of the worksheet.

It obscures your worksheet data, so you need to move it. To do this, click on a

blank part of it and drag it down and to the right to a clear part of the worksheet.

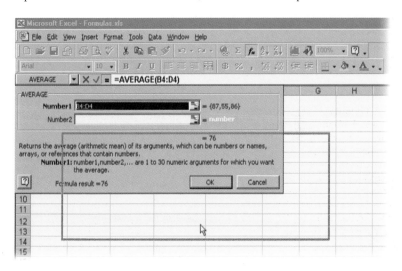

● This dialog box contains two text boxes, **Number1** and **Number2**. These are for entering the arguments of your function – in this case, the range of cells for which you want to calculate the average. In this case, only one argument is required – the cell range **B4:D4**, to be placed in the **Number1** box. In fact, Excel has already guessed that this is the range you want, so just click on **OK**.

● To calculate the other three candidates' averages, just select cell E4 and use the fill handle to copy the formula it contains (=**AVERAGE(B4:D4)**) down to cell E7.

E4	▼	=	=AVERAGE(B4:D4)		
	A	B	C	D	E	F
1	Science exam scores					
2						
3		Physics (%)	Biology (%)	Chemistry (%)	Average	
4	Anne	98	72	95	88.33333333	
5	Bill	71	66	85		
6	Cheryl	58	75	63		
7	Dan	81	84	90		
8	Total	308	297	333		
9						

● The result should be as shown at the right.

| File | Edit | View | Insert | Format | Tools | Data | Window | Help |

Arial ▼ 10 ▼ **B** *I* U ≡ ≡ ≡ 圉 $ % , .00 .00

M28	▼	=	
	A	B	C	D	E	F
1	Science exam scores					
2						
3		Physics (%)	Biology (%)	Chemistry (%)	Average	
4	Anne	98	72	95	88.33333333	
5	Bill	71	66	85	74	
6	Cheryl	58	75	63	65.33333333	
7	Dan	81	84	90	85	
8	Total	308	297	333		
9						

FUNCTION FINDING

Excel functions fall into several categories, such as mathematical functions, statistical functions, and text functions. These categories can help you find useful functions via the **Paste Function** dialog box. If you know the name of a function that you want to use but don't know its category, choose **All** under **Function category**, and then scroll through the full list of functions.

COLLAPSIBLE DIALOG BOX

The second dialog box that appears when you use the **Paste Function** command (the one in which the function's arguments have to be entered) contains buttons decorated with tiny red arrows. Clicking on one of these arrows collapses the box to a single text box, so that it no longer obscures the worksheet data. Once an argument has been entered into the text box, click on a similar button located at the right-hand end of the text box to restore the full dialog box.

2 THE CORREL FUNCTION

● Now try a more challenging task. The **CORREL** function compares two sets of data (such as exam scores on two different subjects) and tests how strongly they are linked or correlated. It calculates a value (the correlation coefficient) that can range from 0 (no correlation) to 1 or -1 (strong positive or negative correlation).

● In cell A12, enter the text shown below, then select cell C12 and click on the **Paste Function** button.

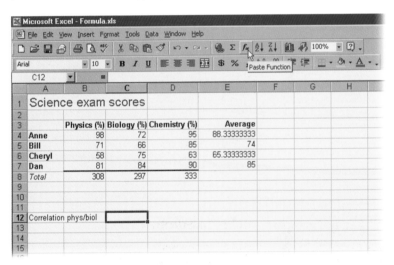

● In the **Paste Function** dialog box, choose **Statistical** under **Function category** and **CORREL** from the **Function name** list. Click on **OK**.

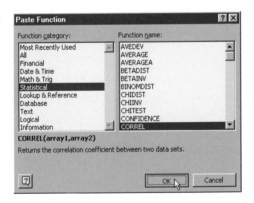

● The dialog box appears for entering the arguments for the **CORREL** function. This time, the Excel program hasn't guessed what arguments you might want to enter. The arguments you need, to be placed in the **Array1** and **Array2** text boxes, are the two ranges of cell values to be compared. In this instance, you want to compare the physics and biology scores.

Shortcut to Functions
A quick way of activating the **Paste Function** command (Function Wizard) is by using the keyboard shortcut
⟨⇧ Shift⟩ and F3.

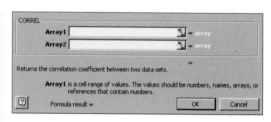

● Click in the **Array1** text box and then drag the mouse pointer over the range B4:B7 to put the range of physics scores in that text box.

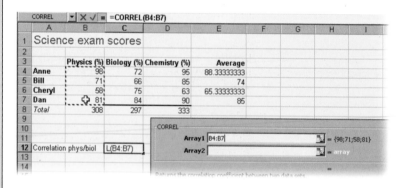

● Now click in the **Array2** text box and then drag the mouse pointer over the range C4:C7 to put all the biology scores in that text box. Click **OK**.

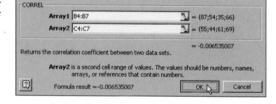

● The physics/biology correlation coefficient comes out close to zero. This indicates that there is no apparent link between the candidates' scores in physics and biology.

8	Total	300	297	393
9		
10		
11		
12	Correlation phys/biol	0.0711235
13		
14		
15		
16		

● Repeat the process, this time comparing the physics and chemistry scores. This time, the correlation coefficient comes out close to 1, indicating a strong link.

9		
10		
11		
12	Correlation phys/biol	0.0711235
13	Correlation phys/chem	0.9077157
14		
15		
16		

A FINANCIAL FUNCTION

Within the **Financial** category of Excel functions are some tools that are likely to be understood only by professional tax advisers and accountants. But others are potentially useful to anyone. Here, you'll look at a function that can be used to work out the monthly payments of interest and capital on a standard type of loan.

1 CALCULATING REPAYMENTS

● Joe Wizzkidd is thinking about taking out an $85,000 loan to buy an apartment. He wants to find out what a monthly repayment might be on a 120-month loan.

● In the **Formula.xls** workbook, choose **Worksheet** from the **Insert** menu. Name it **Loan** and enter the labels and figures shown at the right.

	N28	▼	=		
	A	B	C	D	E
1	Repayment of loan by constant monthly payments				
2	**Amount of loan:**		$85,000.00		
3	**Monthly interest rate**		0.40%		
4	**Term (months)**		120		
5	**Monthly repayments**				
6					
7					
8					
9					

● To calculate the monthly payments, you need to use a financial function called **PMT**. Select cell C5, and click on the **Paste Function** button. Choose **Financial** from the **Function category** list, and choose **PMT** from the list of financial functions. Click on **OK**.

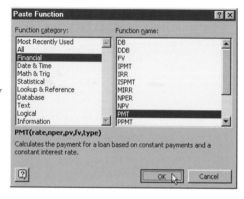

● The **PMT** function requires five arguments. The first, to go into the top text box labeled **Rate**, is the interest rate per period for the loan (in this case, the monthly interest rate). Just click on cell C3, which holds this information. Then press Tab to move to the next text box.

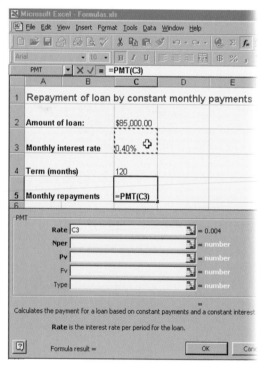

● The next argument required, to go in the text box labeled **Nper**, is the total number of payments for the loan. This is the same as the term of the loan in months. Click on cell C4 and then press Tab to move to the next text box.

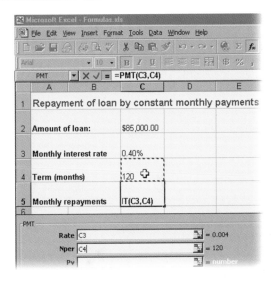

● The third argument, to go in the text box labeled **Pv**, is the "present value." This is simply the loan amount. Click on cell C2 and then press Tab.

● The fourth argument is the "cash balance you want to attain after the last payment is made." This is 0 – once the last payment has been made, Joe wants the whole loan to have been paid off. So type **0** and press [Tab]. In the final text box (**Type**), just type 0. Then press [Enter ↵].

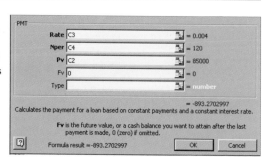

● The PMT function has calculated that Joe will have to make monthly payments of $893.27 to pay the loan off over 120 months. The figure is shown as a negative amount (in red, and parentheses) because it represents a financial outgoing.

	A	B	C	D	E	F
1	Repayment of loan by constant monthly payments					
2	**Amount of loan:**		$85,000.00			
3	**Monthly interest rate**		0.40%			
4	**Term (months)**		120			
5	**Monthly repayments**		($893.27)			
6						

2 ALTERING THE LOAN DETAILS

● Joe thinks that $893.27 per month might overstretch him financially. He decides to look at what the payments might be if he borrowed less ($75,000) and extended the repayment period to 180 months.

● Change the amount of the loan, in cell C2, to **$75,000**. Alter the term of the loan, in months, held in C4, to **180** months. These two changes bring the monthly payment down to $585.31.

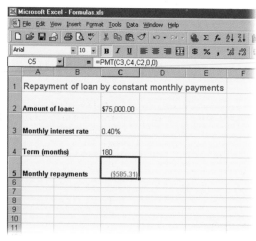

● As a final precaution, Joe wants to test what might happen to his monthly payments should the interest rates rise to, say, 0.6%. He changes the figure in cell C3 to **0.6%** and presses Enter↵.

C3	▼	X √ =	0.6%		
	A	B	C	D	E	F
1	Repayment of loan by constant monthly payments				
2	**Amount of loan:**		$75,000.00		
3	**Monthly interest rate**		0.6%		
4	**Term (months)**		180		
5	**Monthly repayments**		($585.31)		
6					
7					

● With a monthly interest rate of 0.6%, the monthly payments will rise to $682.54, but this is not as bad as Joe had feared. He decides to proceed with his application for a $75,000 loan repayable over 180 months.

Microsoft Excel - Formulas.xls

File Edit View Insert Format Tools Data Window Help

Arial ▼ 10 ▼ **B** *I* U ≡ ≡ ≡ 国 $ % , .00 .00

C4	▼	=	180		
	A	B	C	D	E	F
1	Repayment of loan by constant monthly payments				
2	**Amount of loan:**		$75,000.00		
3	**Monthly interest rate**		0.60%		
4	**Term (months)**		180		
5	**Monthly repayments**		($682.54)		
6					
7					

HIDDEN WORKINGS

When using a function such as **PMT**, the underlying and often complex math involved are completely hidden from view. This is intentional – Excel functions are designed to supply answers to problems without troubling users with the details. But before using an unfamiliar function, be sure you fully understand what its arguments are.

RECENTLY USED FUNCTIONS

To speed up the process of calling up functions for placing in formulas, Excel provides a recently-used function list. To use this list, after selecting the cell into which you want to put a formula, click on the **Edit Formula** button (the = sign to the left of the formula bar).

The name of the most recently used function then appears to the far left of the formula bar. You will see a small downward-pointing arrow to the right of this. Clicking on the arrow drops down a list of the 10 most recently used functions.

ASSORTED FUNCTIONS

Excel 2000 offers more than 230 different functions for use in worksheets, and even more functions are available as an "add-in" or extension to the program called the Analysis Toolpak. Try out the following functions to give you a flavor of some of the other types of calculation and manipulation tools available.

1 FINDING THE WEEKDAY

● The **WEEKDAY** function tells you the day of the week for any date between January 1, 1900 and December 31, 9999. Suppose, for example, that you are researching the mission of Apollo 11, the first manned lunar landing. You know that the module touched down on the Moon on July 20, 1969, but you want to know what day of the week that happened.

● In the **Formula.xls** workbook, choose **Worksheet** from the **Insert** menu to create a new worksheet. Name it **Morefunctions**. In cell B2, type 20 Jul 1969. Excel will recognize this as a date.

CONSTRUCTING ROMAN NUMERALS

If you have trouble understanding how to construct Roman numerals from Arabic ones, you might wish to look at the Excel function, **ROMAN**. You can use this function to convert an Arabic numeral into a Roman one. Excel does not provide, however, a tool for the reverse operation of translating a Roman numeral into an Arabic one.

● Select cell C2, and then use the **Paste Function** button to call up the function **WEEKDAY** (it is in the list of **Date & Time** functions). Click on **OK**. In the top text box, labeled **Serial_number**, enter the cell reference for your date, **B2**. Then press Tab.

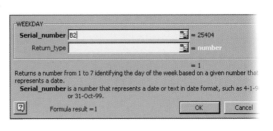

● In the lower text box, labeled **Return_type,** type a **2**. This indicates that you want days of the week coded from Monday through Sunday with the numbers 1–7. Press Enter←.

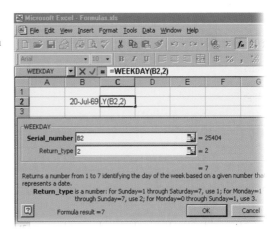

● The number returned is a 7, indicating that humans first visited the Moon on a Sunday.

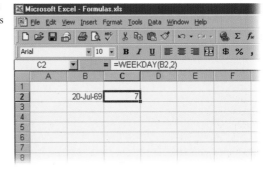

2 RANDOM NUMBERS

● Suppose you want to create a series of random numbers between, say, 1 and 60, perhaps for a lottery entry. The Excel function **RAND** will generate a random decimal number between 0 and 1.

● In your **Morefunctions** worksheet, widen column B to about twice normal width and enter the formula =**60*RAND**() into cell B4.

● Press Enter↵ and you will see a randomly generated number, normally 9 or 10 digits long (including the figures after the decimal point), that is greater than 0 but less than 60. It will be a different number from the one shown at right, but it will have the same form.

● Press the F9 key a few times. With each press, you'll see your number change. Pressing the F9 key forces the **RAND** function to generate a new random number with each press.

● To convert the generated numbers into integers (whole numbers), use the **ROUNDUP** function. Select cell C4, and use the **Paste Function** button to call up **ROUNDUP** (it is in the **Math & Trig** category). Click on **OK**.

● In the top text box of the **ROUNDUP** dialog box, labeled **Number**, enter **B4** (the cell that contains the number you want to round up). Press Tab and enter a **0** in the lower text box (indicating that you want to round up to a whole number). Then click **OK**.

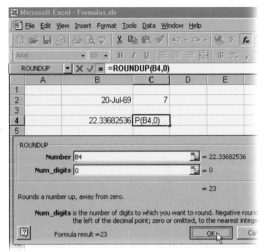

● Press the F9 key repeatedly to obtain random numbers between 1 and 60 in cell C4. With each press, each of the numbers between 1 and 60 (inclusive) has an equal chance of appearing next.

B	C
20-Jul-69	7
57.3533551	58

B	C
20-Jul-69	7
17.73253546	18

MORE MATH FUNCTIONS

The **Math & Trig** category of Excel functions include a large number of calculation tools of the type you would expect to find in an extremely sophisticated electronic calculator. These calculation tools include logarithmic functions such as **LOG** and **LN**, trigonometric functions such as **COS**, **SIN**, and **TAN**, the function **RADIAN** for converting degrees to radians, and **FACT** for finding the factorial of a number.

3 A LOGICAL FUNCTION

● In the **Logical** category of Excel functions are tools that will apply various tests to a worksheet and return different values depending on the test results. The simplest is the **IF** function, which applies a single test and returns one of two possible values, depending on whether the result of the test is positive or negative. Try this simple example to see how it works.

● Type the text labels and numbers shown below into the cell range A7:C14 of your **Morefunctions** worksheet. Let's suppose that you want to assign an "A" or a "B" grade to each person's exam score depending on whether it is above or below 90.

	N31	▼	=						
	A	B	C	D	E	F	G	H	I
1									
2		20-Jul-69	7						
3									
4		17.73253546	18						
5									
6									
7		Score	Grade						
8	Grace	97							
9	Michael	80							
10	Kym	93							
11	Bradley	87							
12	Amy	85							
13	Frances	81							
14	Harry	94							
15									

● Select cell C8, and use the **Paste Function** button to call up the function **IF** from the **Logical** function category.
● In the top text box, labeled **Logical_test**, type B8>90. This means "look at cell B8 and decide whether its value is greater than 90, or not." Then press Tab.

		Score	Grade
7		Score	Grade
8	Grace	97	(B8>90)
9	Michael	80	
10	Kym	93	
11	Bradley	87	
12	Amy	85	
13	Frances	81	
14	Harry	94	

IF

Logical_test   B8>90   = TRUE

Value_if_true   = any

Value_if_false   = any

=

Returns one value if a condition you specify evaluates to TRUE and another val evaluates to FALSE.

Logical_test is any value or expression that can be evaluated to TRUE o

● In the **Value_if_true** box, type **A**. Press Tab, and in the **Value_if_false** box, type **B**. Then press Enter ←. Click on **OK**.

		Score		Grade	
5					
6					
7		Score		Grade	
8	Grace	97		),"A",B)	
9	Michael	80			
10	Kym	93			
11	Bradley	87			
12	Amy	85			
13	Frances	81			
14	Harry	94			
15					

IF		
Logical_test	B8>90	= TRUE
Value_if_true	"A"	= "A"
Value_if_false	B	=

● The value returned in cell C8 is A because Grace's score is greater than 90. Now copy the formula in C8 down to the six cells below it.

		Score	Grade
5			
6			
7		Score	Grade
8	Grace	97	A
9	Michael	80	
10	Kym	93	
11	Bradley	87	
12	Amy	85	
13	Frances	81	
14	Harry	94	
15			

● The scores have now all been automatically graded.

		Score	Grade
7		Score	Grade
8	Grace	97	A
9	Michael	80	B
10	Kym	93	A
11	Bradley	87	B
12	Amy	85	B
13	Frances	81	B
14	Harry	94	A

TEXT MANIPULATION

In the **TEXT** function category are tools that can be used to measure and manipulate strings of text characters. For example, **LEFT** will extract a specified number of letters at the beginning of a text string. **TRIM** will remove all spaces from a string of text except for single spaces between words. **REPLACE** will replace part of a text string with another text string.

WORKSHEET ERRORS

As you use more formulas in your worksheets, you'll occasionally construct one that Excel cannot understand. Here, we explain the source of such problems and how to resolve them.

SOURCES OF ERRORS

There are many different ways of ending up with a formula that Excel cannot process or understand. When an error occurs, Excel carries out some analysis of the problem and then displays an error value, such as #DIV/0! or #VALUE!, in the affected cell. The type of error value displayed is intended to give some indication of the cause of the problem. Overall, there are some eight or nine different error values, of which the most common are covered here. Others, such as #NULL!, are likely to be encountered only by more advanced Excel users.

1 A #DIV/0! ERROR

● The #DIV/0! error value occurs when a formula divides something by 0 (zero), which is a mathematical absurdity. The usual cause is the use of a reference to a blank cell or one with a value of zero as the divisor in a formula.

● In a new worksheet called **Errors**, enter the text labels and numbers shown at right. The worksheet shows some scores from the obscure sport of smashball.

Player	Hits	Misses	HMR (Hit/Miss ratio)	Star rating
Avery	39	5		
Bransky	96	6		
Coppi	12	0		
Darcy	22	8		
Total	169	19		

● A key statistic in smashball is the ratio of "goal hits" to "goal misses," also called the HMR (hit/miss ratio). To calculate the first player's HMR, enter the formula =**B3/C3** in cell D3. Press Enter↵ .

	A	B	C	D	E
1	Smashball statistics				
2	Player	Hits	Misses	HMR (Hit/Miss ratio)	Star rating
3	Avery	39	5	=B3/C3	
4	Bransky	96	6		
5	Coppi	12	0		
6	Darcy	22	8		
7	Total	169	19		

● Copy the formula down through cells D4 to D6. A **#DIV/0!** error value is generated in cell D5. This is because it contains the formula =B5/C5, and the value of cell C5, the divisor, is 0.

M26			=		
	A	B	C	D	E
1	Smashball statistics				
2	Player	Hits	Misses	HMR (Hit/Miss ratio)	Star rating
3	Avery	39	5	7.8	
4	Bransky	96	6	16	
5	Coppi	12	0	#DIV/0!	
6	Darcy	22	8	2.75	
7	Total	169	19		
8					

● It is discovered that the player named Coppi actually had 2 misses. Change the value of cell C5 to **2**, and the #DIV/0! error disappears.

	A	B	C	D	E
1	Smashball statistics				
2	Player	Hits	Misses	HMR (Hit/Miss ratio)	Star rating
3	Avery	39	5	7.8	
4	Bransky	96	6	16	
5	Coppi	12	2	6	
6	Darcy	22	8	2.75	
7	Total	169	21		

WHAT DOES ###### MEAN?

If you see the expression ##### in a cell, this means it contains a number, date, or time that is wider than the cell or that the cell contains a date and/or time formula that produces a negative result. Try widening the column. If that doesn't work, and if there is a formula in the cell, check the validity of the formula. For example, subtracting a date or time from an earlier date or time would cause the ##### error. If the cell is supposed to contain a negative number, make sure the cell does not have a date or time format.

2 A #NUM! ERROR

● The #NUM! error value occurs as a result of a formula that cannot be calculated (other than dividing by zero) or that generates a number that is too large or small for Excel to handle or display. Try this example.

● The star rating of a smashball player is found by subtracting 3 from his or her HMR, taking the square root of the result, and rounding down. To find the first player's star rating, enter the formula =**TRUNC(SQRT(D3-3))** in cell E3 (the function **TRUNC** rounds down to the nearest whole number). Press Enter↵.

MIN ▾ X ✓ = =TRUNC(SQRT(D3-3))

Smashball statistics

	A	B	C	D	E	F
1	Smashball statistics					
2	Player	Hits	Misses	HMR (Hit/Miss ratio)	Star rating	
3	Avery	39	5		=TRUNC(SQRT(D3-3))	
4	Bransky	96	6	16		
5	Coppi	12	2	6		
6	Darcy	22	8	2.75		
7	Total	169	21			

● Copy the formula from cell E3 down through cells E4 to E6.

Smashball statistics

	A	B	C	D	E	F
1	Smashball statistics					
2	Player	Hits	Misses	HMR (Hit/Miss ratio)	Star rating	
3	Avery	39	5	7.8	2	
4	Bransky	96	6	16		
5	Coppi	12	2	6		
6	Darcy	22	8	2.75		
7	Total	169	21			

● A #NUM! error value appears in cell E6 because the formula in cell E6 asked Excel to find the square root of a negative number, and there are no real square roots of negative numbers.

	Player	Hits	Misses	HMR (Hit/Miss ratio)	Star rating
2	Player	Hits	Misses	HMR (Hit/Miss ratio)	Star rating
3	Avery	39	5	7.8	2
4	Bransky	96	6	16	3
5	Coppi	12	2	6	1
6	Darcy	22	8	2.75	#NUM!
7	Total	169	21		

● Since the player called Darcy has a star rating that is incalculable, count it as zero by changing the contents of cell E6 to 0.

	A	B	C	D	E	F
1	Smashball statistics					
2	Player	Hits	Misses	HMR (Hit/Miss ratio)	Star rating	
3	Avery	39	5	7.8	2	
4	Bransky	96	6	16	3	
5	Coppi	12	2	6	1	
6	Darcy	22	8	2.75	0	
7	Total	169	21			
8						
9						

3 A #VALUE! ERROR

● The #VALUE! error occurs as a result of the wrong type of operand being used in a formula or the wrong type of argument being used for a function, for example, using text in a formula that requires a number, or supplying a range of cells for a function that requires a single value.

● In cell A9, enter the text **Total goal attempts**, and in cell C9, enter the formula **=A7+B7**. Press Enter ↵.

Microsoft Excel - Formulas.xls

File Edit View Insert Format Tools Data Window Help

Arial · 10 · B I U

MIN ▾ X ✔ = =A7+B7

	A	B	C	D	E	F
1	Smashball statistics					
2	Player	Hits	Misses	HMR (Hit/Miss ratio)	Star rating	
3	Avery	39	5	7.8	2	
4	Bransky	96	6	16	3	
5	Coppi	12	2	6	1	
6	Darcy	22	8	2.75	0	
7	Total	169	21			
8						
9	Total goal attempts:	=A7+B7				
10						
11						
12						

● A #VALUE! error is generated. That is because the formula you typed in adds a text value (Total in cell A7) to a number value (169 in cell B7). Excel cannot make sense of this. The formula you entered in cell C9 should have been =B7+C7, but leave it as it is for now.

	A	B	C	D	E	F
1	Smashball statistics					
2	Player	Hits	Misses	HMR (Hit/Miss ratio)	Star rating	
3	Avery	39	5	7.8	2	
4	Bransky	96	6	16	3	
5	Coppi	12	2	6	1	
6	Darcy	22	8	2.75	0	
7	Total	169	21			
8						
9	Total goal attempts:		#VALUE!			
10						
11						

4 A CIRCULAR REFERENCE ERROR

● A circular reference error occurs when a cell reference within a formula refers back, directly or indirectly, to the cell containing the formula. The best way of understanding how such an error occurs is to generate an example.

● In your **Errors** worksheet, enter the labels **Factor X**, **Factor Y**, and **Factor Z** in cells A11, C11, and B13 as shown. In cell A12 (Factor X), enter the value **5**. In cell C12 (Factor Y), enter the formula =**A12*6**.

Microsoft Excel - Formulas.xls

File Edit View Insert Format Tools Data Window Help

MIN ▼ X ✓ = =A12*6

	A	B	C	D	E	F
1	Smashball statistics					
2	Player	Hits	Misses	HMR (Hit/Miss ratio)	Star rating	
3	Avery	39	5	7.8	2	
4	Bransky	96	6	16	3	
5	Coppi	12	2	6	1	
6	Darcy	22	8	2.75	0	
7	Total	169	21			
8						
9	Total goal attempts:		#VALUE!			
10						
11	Factor X		Factor Y			
12	5		=A12*6			
13			Factor Z			
14						
15						
16						
17						

● In cell B14 (Factor Z), enter the formula =**C12-10**. Then double-click on cell A12 (Factor X again) and change its contents to the formula =**B14+22**.

	A	B	C
9	Total goal attempts:	#VALUE!	
10			
11	Factor X		Factor Y
12	=B14+22		30
13		Factor Z	
14		20	
15			

● Press Enter←. An error message box appears telling you that Excel cannot calculate a formula. That is because the formula you put in cell A12 refers to the value in cell B14; this contains a formula that refers to the value in C12, and C12 in turn contains a formula that refers back to the value in A12!

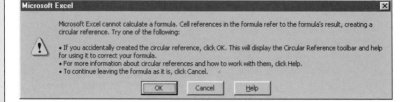

Microsoft Excel ✕

⚠ Microsoft Excel cannot calculate a formula. Cell references in the formula refer to the formula's result, creating a circular reference. Try one of the following:

• If you accidentally created the circular reference, click OK. This will display the Circular Reference toolbar and help for using it to correct your formula.
• For more information about circular references and how to work with them, click Help.
• To continue leaving the formula as it is, click Cancel.

[OK] [Cancel] [Help]

● For a visual representation of the error, click **Cancel** in the message box (you will see that Excel just stores a "0" for the time being in cell A12). Then choose **Toolbars** from the **View** menu and **Circular Reference** from the submenu.

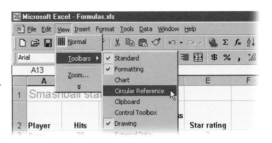

● Three arrows appear on your worksheet, illustrating the series of references that make up the circular reference. A **Circular Reference** toolbar also appears. You should also see a message **Circular:B14** in the status bar at the foot of your Excel window.

● Clicking on the down arrow within the **Circular Reference** toolbar reveals a list of the cells involved in the circular reference – B14, C12, and A12. You can choose any cell in the list in order to view and possibly correct the formula it contains. For now, just close the toolbar.

#NAME? ERROR

The #NAME? error value occurs when Excel doesn't recognize text in a formula. Some common causes include misspelling the names of functions, omitting the colon (:) in references to cell ranges, or forgetting to enclose text used in formulas in double quotation marks.

EXCEL'S AUDITING TOOLS

Excel provides a number of tools to assist in tracing the source of errors. A cell that displays an error value causes any cells that reference it – called its dependent cells – to display the error as well. So, when a formula containing cell references gives rise to an error value, the problem may arise in the formula itself or in one of the cells referred to, which are called its precedent cells. If a worksheet contains a complex chain of formulas and a crop of error values appears, tracing the source of the problem can be time-consuming. Excel's auditing commands, which include the trace precedents tool, the trace dependents tool, and the trace error tool, can simplify the process. Let's take a look at two of these tools.

1 THE TRACE PRECEDENTS TOOL

● The trace precedents tool visually indicates the precedents of a given cell i.e., any cells referred to by a formula within that cell.

• First change the formula in cell A12 to =C9*B3. When you press R, you will see a #VALUE! error appear in cell A12, and also in its dependent cells, C12 and B14.

	A	B	C	D	E
1	Smashball statistics				
2	Player	Hits	Misses	HMR (Hit/Miss ratio)	Star rating
3	Avery	39	5	7.8	2
4	Bransky	96	6	16	3
5	Coppi	12	2	6	1
6	Darcy	22	8	2.75	0
7	Total	169	21		
8					
9	Total goal attempts:		#VALUE!		
10					
11	Factor X		Factor Y		
12	=C9*B3		30		
13		Factor Z			
14		20			
15					

● Now select cell A12, choose **Auditing** from the **Tools** menu, and **Trace Precedents** from the submenu.

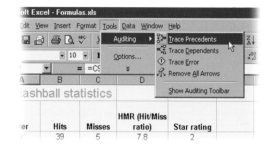

● Two arrows appear on the worksheet pointing from A12's precedent cells (B3 and C9) to A12 itself. The red arrow from C9 to A12 indicates that C9 itself contains an error value. Plainly, the error value in cell A12 can be traced at least as far back as cell C9. To remove the arrows, go to the **Tools** menu, choose **Auditing,** and click on **Remove All Arrows**.

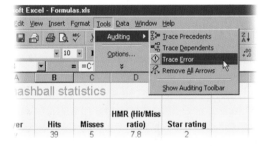

2 THE TRACE ERROR TOOL

● The most useful Excel auditing tool is the trace error tool. This can only be used when the selected cell contains an error value.

● Select cell B14 and then choose **Auditing** from the **Tools** menu and **Trace Error** from the submenu.

● Several red arrows lead to cell B14 from the first of its precedent cells that contains an error (cell C9). Cell C9 has also become the active cell, and its own precedents are indicated by blue arrows. The source of the crop of errors on the worksheet is clearly cell C9. This cell contains an uncorrected formula that attempts to multiply a text value by a number.

GLOSSARY

ABSOLUTE CELL REFERENCE
See Cell Reference.

ACTIVE CELL
On a worksheet, the active cell has a thick, black border around it. In a selected block of cells, it will be the white cell. The active cell can be moved by pointing and clicking with the mouse or by using the [Enter ↵], [Tab], or cursor arrow keys.

ARGUMENT
A piece of data required by a function in order to perform its particular task. An argument of a function may be the value in a specific cell or the values in a range of cells, or a number or a piece of text you provide. Different functions vary in the number of arguments they need.

CELL RANGE
A rectangular block of cells in a worksheet. For example, the range B1:D5 means the block of 15 cells that have the cells B1 and D5 at opposite corners.

CELL REFERENCE
An expression within a formula used to signify the value within a specific cell. For example, the cell reference "$A$2" within a formula in cell D2 means "the value in cell A2." There are two types of cell reference: relative and absolute. The reference "$A$2" is an absolute reference and always refers to cell A2, wherever it is copied in the worksheet. A cell reference "A2" within D2, on the other hand, would be a relative cell reference

and really means "the cell three to the left of this one." Relative cell references adjust when they are copied to other cells.

CELL VALUE
What you see in a cell on-screen. A value can be numerical, such as a number or a date, or a text value. There is a distinction between constant values, which are never affected when other cell values change; and variable values, which are calculated by formulas that refer to other cells. Variable values change when the value of the referenced cells change.

ERROR VALUE
A cell value, such as #DIV/0! or #NUM!, that indicates a cell contains a formula that Excel cannot understand or calculate.

FORMULA
An expression entered into a cell that calculates its value from a combination of constants, operators, and the values of other cells in the worksheet. All formulas start with the "=" character. A formula can also contain one or more functions.

FORMULA BAR
The white bar above the work-sheet that always displays the contents of the active cell, either a formula or constant value. The contents of the active cell can be edited in the formula bar.

FUNCTION
A named, ready-formed, calculation tool that can be incorporated into a formula

and carries out a specific operation on some data. For example, the AVERAGE function calculates the average (or mean) of a list of numbers. Most functions require some specific pieces of data to be supplied – these are called the function's arguments. A few functions require no arguments.

LINK
A connection between two cells created by entering a formula in one cell that contains a reference to the other cell. The two cells may be in the same worksheet, different worksheets within the same workbook, or even in different workbooks.

OPERATOR
A character entered into a formula that signifies a specific type of arithmetic or other operation. The main arithmetic operators are + (signifying addition), - (subtraction), * (multiplication), / (division), and ^ (raising to a power). A commonly-used nonarithmetic operator is the ampersand (&), which joins two pieces of text.

OPERAND
Pieces of data that are operated upon, combined, or manipulated by a formula. The operands are usually numbers or other types of data that have been typed into the formula, or are references to other worksheet cells.

RELATIVE CELL REFERENCE
See Cell Reference.